SCHOLASTIC

Learning Express

English

Phonics and Reading Skills

This book belongs to

_____

For information regarding permission, write to:
Scholastic Education International (Singapore) Pte Ltd
81 Ubi Avenue 4, #02-28 UB.ONE, Singapore 408830
Email: education@scholastic.com.sg

For sales enquiries write to:
Latin America, Caribbean, Europe (except UK), Middle East and Africa
Scholastic International
557 Broadway, New York, NY 10012, USA
Email: intlschool@scholastic.com

Philippines
Scholastic Philippines
Penthouse 1, Prestige Tower, F. Ortigas Jr. Road,
Ortigas Center, Pasig City 1605
Email: educteam@scholastic.com.ph

Asia (excluding India and Philippines)
Scholastic Asia
Plaza First Nationwide, 161, Jalan Tun H S Lee,
50000 Kuala Lumpur, Wilayah Persekutuan Kuala Lumpur, Malaysia
Email: international@scholastic.com

Rest of the World
Scholastic Education International (Singapore) Pte Ltd
81 Ubi Avenue 4 #02-28 UB.ONE Singapore 408830
Email: education@scholastic.com.sg

Australia
Scholastic Australia Pty Ltd
PO Box 579, Gosford, NSW 2250
Email: scholastic_education@scholastic.com.au

New Zealand
Scholastic New Zealand Ltd
Private Bag 94407, Botany, Auckland 2163
Email: orders@scholastic.co.nz

India
Scholastic India Pvt. Ltd.
A-27, Ground Floor, Bharti Sigma Centre,
Infocity-1, Sector 34, Gurgaon (Haryana) 122001, India
Email: education@scholastic.co.in

Visit our website: www.scholastic.com.sg

First edition 2013
Reprinted 2018

ISBN 978-981-07-1363-8

Welcome to Learning Express!

Helping your child build essential skills is easy!

These teacher-approved activities have been specially developed to make learning both accessible and enjoyable. On each page, you'll find:

Focus skill
The focus of each activity page is clearly indicated.

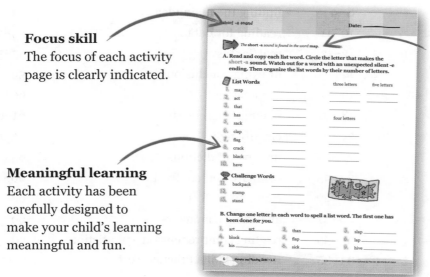

Instructions
The read-aloud instructions are easy for your child to understand.

Meaningful learning
Each activity has been carefully designed to make your child's learning meaningful and fun.

This book also contains:

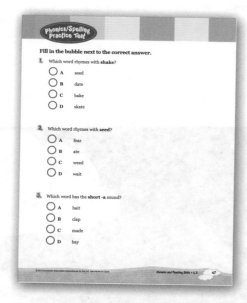

Instant assessment to ensure your child really masters the skills.

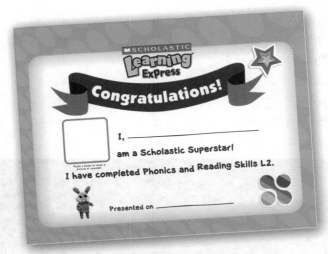

Completion certificate to celebrate your child's leap in learning.

Motivational stickers to mark the milestones of your child's learning path.

Contents

© 2013 Scholastic Education International (S) Pte Ltd ISBN 978-981-07-1363-8

Phonics/Spelling

"Look, Mom, I can read it all by myself!" What a proud moment for your child. Understanding the relationship between letters and the sounds they make is the most important step in learning how to read. In this section, children use their knowledge of phonics to develop spelling skills.

What To Do

These activities provide practice in the spelling of rhyming words, vowel and consonant sounds and unusual spellings of certain sounds.

Read the definition of the skill to your child. Then have him or her complete the activity. Help your child check the work when finished.

Keep On Going!

Play a word game with your child. Tell him or her, I am thinking of a word:

> It starts with a *k* sound.
> It has a short -*a* in the middle.
> It ends with a *t* sound.
> It rhymes with *fat*.
> What is the word? [cat]
> How do you spell it?

Date: _____

 The **short -a** *sound is found in the word* **map**.

A. Read and copy each list word. Circle the letter that makes the short -a sound. Watch out for a word with an unexpected silent -e ending. Then organize the list words by their number of letters.

List Words

			three letters	five letters
1.	map	_____	_____	_____
2.	act	_____	_____	_____
3.	that	_____	_____	
4.	has	_____	four letters	
5.	sack	_____	_____	
6.	clap	_____	_____	
7.	flag	_____	_____	
8.	crack	_____	_____	
9.	black	_____	_____	
10.	have	_____		

Challenge Words

11. backpack _____
12. stamp _____
13. stand _____

B. Change one letter in each word to spell a list word. The first one has been done for you.

1. art ___act___
2. than _____
3. slap _____
4. block _____
5. flap _____
6. lap _____
7. his _____
8. sick _____
9. hive _____

A. Use the list words to complete the story.

Matt's Map

Matt _____ a map of the houses on his street. He keeps the map in his

_____ sack. But _____ night Matt could not find his map. He looked

everywhere. "Do you _____ my map?" he would ask everyone. Matt saw

something under his Halloween mask. It was his _____! Matt was so happy

he began to _____. After that, Matt always put his map back in his black

_____.

B. Follow the clues to play tic-tac-toe. As you find each answer, mark an X or O. Do you get three in a row?

1. He would love to _____ in the play. Mark an **X**.
2. I am a color. Mark an **O**.
3. I rhyme with **chat**. Mark an **X**.
4. I mean the same as **break**. Mark an **O**.
5. She _____ a sister. Mark an **X**.
6. I begin like the word **sit**. Mark an **O**.
7. I rhyme with **map**. Mark an **X**.
8. They _____ a dog. Mark an **O**.
9. I rhyme with **bag**. Mark an **X**.

has	have	clap
black	flag	sack
that	crack	act

C. Write the challenge word that finishes each analogy.

1. You put a plate on the table. You put a _____ on a letter.
2. **Down** is the antonym for **up**. **Sit** is the antonym for _____.
3. A wallet is kept in a purse. A book is kept in a _____.

Date: _____

 *The **short -e** sound is found in the word **tent**.*

A. Read and copy each list word. Circle the letter that makes the short -e sound. Watch out for a word with an unexpected spelling. Then organize the list words by their ending letters.

List Words

			words that end with **t**	words that end with **d**
1.	tent	_____	_____	_____
2.	met	_____	_____	_____
3.	send	_____	_____	_____
4.	went	_____	_____	_____
5.	bed	_____		
6.	nest	_____	_____	
7.	bend	_____	_____	
8.	yet	_____	_____	
9.	best	_____		
10.	said	_____		

Challenge Words

11.	bench	_____
12.	next	_____
13.	else	_____

B. Each list word has a rhyming partner. Write two list words that rhyme.

1. _____ 2. _____ 3. _____

_____   _____   _____

4. _____ 5. _____

_____   _____

Date: _____

Circle ten misspelled words. Write them correctly on the lines.

My Backyard Tent

My dad and I built a tint in the backyard. We had to bind
sticks to stake it in the ground. We had the beste time. We
made a bid out of straw. We sed it was like a bird's nast.
My mom said she would sind a snack out to us. We mete
her in the yard and then she whent back in the house.
She said she isn't ready for camping yat!

1. _____   2. _____   3. _____   4. _____

5. _____   6. _____   7. _____   8. _____

9. _____   10. _____

Use addition and subtraction to spell each list word. The first one has been done for you.

11. rest – r + b = _____best_____   12. test – s + n = _____

13. mat – a + e = _____   14. bad – a + e = _____

15. sent – t + d = _____   16. sand – n + i = _____

17. send – s + b = _____   18. set – s + y = _____

19. next – x + s = _____   20. want – a + e = _____

Write the challenge word that matches each definition.

21. another choice _____

22. a place to sit _____

23. the nearest in order _____

Date: _____

 *The **short -i** sound is found in the word **miss**.*

A. Read and copy each list word. Circle the letter that makes the short -i sound. Then organize the list words by the letter clues.

List Words

			words that begin with **m**	words that have a **p**
1.	hid	_____		
2.	mix	_____	_____	_____
3.	with	_____	_____	_____
4.	tip	_____	_____	_____
5.	milk	_____		
6.	miss	_____	words that begin with **k**	words that have an **h**
7.	slip	_____		
8.	kick	_____	_____	_____
9.	kiss	_____	_____	_____
10.	pick	_____		

🏆 Challenge Words

11.	into	_____
12.	trick	_____
13.	sister	_____

B. Circle the word that is spelled correctly.

1.	pik	pick	2.	melk	milk	3.	kiss	kis
4.	tip	tipp	5.	slep	slip	6.	kik	kick
7.	hid	hidd	8.	miks	mix	9.	mis	miss

© 2013 Scholastic Education International (S) Pte Ltd ISBN 978-981-07-1363-8

Date: _____

Write the list word that matches each clue.

1.   I am the past tense of **hide**. I am _____.

2.   We rhyme with **sick**. We are _____ and _____.

3.   I am part of the dairy food group. I am _____.

4.   I begin with the same sound as **wind**. I am _____.

5.   I am a synonym for **stir**. I am _____.

6.   We rhyme with **flip**. We are _____ and _____.

7.   Do this to your mom or dad. This is _____.

8.   I am kiss – k + m. I am _____.

Circle each list word hidden in the puzzle. The words go across, down or diagonally.

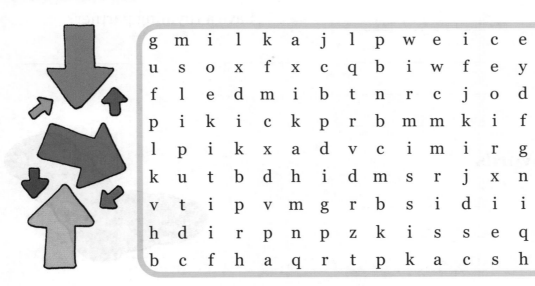

```
g  m  i  l  k  a  j  l  p  w  e  i  c  e  o
u  s  o  x  f  x  c  q  b  i  w  f  e  y  z
f  l  e  d  m  i  b  t  n  r  c  j  o  d  w
p  i  k  i  c  k  p  r  b  m  m  k  i  f  i
l  p  i  k  x  a  d  v  c  i  m  i  r  g  t
k  u  t  b  d  h  i  d  m  s  r  j  x  n  h
v  t  i  p  v  m  g  r  b  s  i  d  i  i  d
h  d  i  r  p  n  p  z  k  i  s  s  e  q  i
b  c  f  h  a  q  r  t  p  k  a  c  s  h  e
```

Write the challenge word that completes each question.

9.   Does Josie's _____ share a bedroom with her?

10.   Did you stir the milk _____ the cake mix?

11.   Have you learned a new magic _____?

 The **short -o** *sound is found in the word* **sock***.*

A. Read and copy each list word. Circle the letter that makes the short -o sound. Then organize the list words in rhyming pairs.

List Words   rhyming pairs

1. sock   _____   _____ _____
2. mop   _____   _____ _____
3. box   _____   _____ _____
4. spot   _____   _____ _____
5. odd   _____
6. off   _____   Which two words do not
7. dot   _____   have a rhyming partner?
8. stop   _____
9. fox   _____   _____ _____
10. lock   _____

Challenge Words

11. clock   _____
12. cross   _____
13. stomp   _____

B. Change the vowel in each word to spell a list word.

1. map _____   2. step _____   3. sack _____
4. fix _____   5. lick _____   6. spit _____
7. add _____

Date: _____

Use a list word to complete each analogy.

1. **Pull** is the antonym for **push**. **On** is the antonym for _____.

2. A hat goes on your head. A _____ goes on your foot.

3. Scrub a pan. _____ a floor.

4. A knob opens a door. A key opens a _____.

5. **An** is in can. **Ox** is in _____ or _____.

6. **Short** is the antonym for **tall**. _____ is the antonym for **go**.

7. Two, four and six are even. One, three and five are _____.

8. A box is square. A _____ is round.

9. A puddle is on the street. A _____ is on the rug.

Complete each puzzle with two list words.

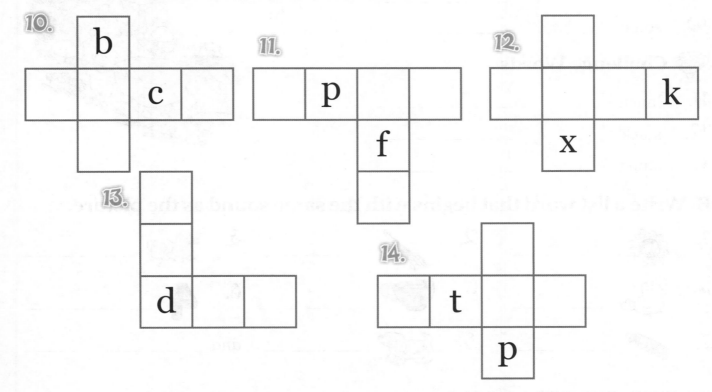

10. b / c

11. p / f

12. k / x

13. d

14. t / p

Date: _____

 The **short -u** *sound is found in the word* **bump**.

A. Read and copy each list word. Circle the letter that makes the short -u sound. Watch for words that use unexpected spellings. Then organize the list by the letters making the short -u sound.

📝 List Words

			u	o
1.	rub	_____	_____	_____
2.	bump	_____	_____	_____
3.	come	_____	_____	**o_e** _____
4.	cut	_____	_____	_____
5.	dump	_____	_____	_____
6.	must	_____	_____	_____
7.	front	_____		
8.	dust	_____		
9.	tub	_____		
10.	some	_____		

🏆 Challenge Words

11.	lunch	_____
12.	stuck	_____
13.	stung	_____

B. Write a list word that begins with the same sound as the picture.

1. _____

2. _____

3. _____

4. _____

5. _____

6. _____

7. _____

8. _____ *and* _____

Date: _____

Use two list words to make a rhyme.

1. We hit a _____ on our way to the _____.

2. Will you give my back a _____ while I sit in the warm _____?

3. Achoo! I really _____ begin to _____.

4. These cookies are great! When I _____, I will bring _____.

Use the clues to identify the list words. Move the jeeps along the road by circling the answers. The jeep that reaches the end of the road first is the winner!

5. more than one

6. a verb that rhymes with **but**

7. a verb that rhymes with **cub**

8. starts like **friend**

9. jump – j + d

10. dirt

11. Change the vowel in **most**.

12. starts like **candy**

13. a noun that rhymes with **cub**

14. a _____ in the road

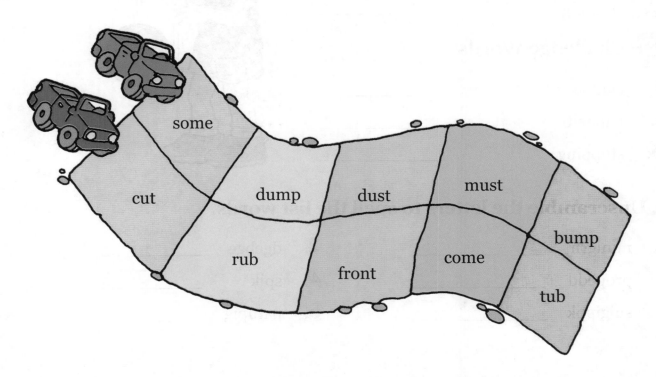

some

cut

dump

dust

must

rub

front

come

bump

tub

Date: _____

*Each of these words has a **short-vowel** spelling with one final consonant. Before adding an ending like **-ing** or **-ed**, double the final consonant.*

A. Read and copy each list word. Circle the letter that makes the short-vowel sound. Underline the words with double consonants.

📝 List Words

			words with no ending	words with an **-ed** ending
1.	tap	_____		
2.	tapping	_____		_____
3.	beg	_____	_____	_____
4.	begged	_____	_____	words with an **-ing** ending
5.	skip	_____	_____	
6.	skipping	_____	_____	_____
7.	drop	_____		_____
8.	dropped	_____		_____
9.	run	_____		
10.	running	_____		

🏆 Challenge Words

11. clapped _____

12. tripped _____

13. stopping _____

B. Unscramble the letters to spell the list words.

1. nunigrn _____

2. dgebge _____

3. propedd _____

4. spik _____

5. snigippk _____

6. patnpig _____

Date: _____

Write four sentences using at least two list words in each.

1. _____
2. _____
3. _____
4. _____

Crack the code to spell each list word.

a	b	d	e	g	i	k	n	o	p	r	s	t	u
☆	✧	✓	⊙	✹	✪	🕐	★	⇧	○	✗	⌛	□	✳

5. ✓ ✗ ⇧ ○ ○ ⊙ ✓ — dropped

6. ⌛ 🕐 ✪ ○ — skip

7. ⌛ 🕐 ✪ ○ ○ ✪ ★ ✹ — skipping

8. ✗ ✳ ★ — run

9. ✗ ✳ ★ ★ ✪ ★ ✹ — running

10. ✓ ✗ ⇧ ○ — drop

11. □ ☆ ○ — tap

12. □ ☆ ○ ○ ✪ ★ ✹ — tapping

13. ✧ ⊙ ✹ ✹ ⊙ ✓ — begged

14. ✧ ⊙ ✹ — beg

The **long -a** *sound can be spelled with the letters* **a_e, ai** *or* **ay***.*

A. Read and copy each list word. Circle the letters that make the long -a sound. Watch out for a word with an unexpected spelling. Then organize the list words by the letters making the long -a sound.

List Words

		a_e	ai
1. say	_____	_____	_____
2. made	_____	_____	_____
3. snake	_____	_____	_____
4. pain	_____	_____	
5. away	_____		**ay**
6. trade	_____	unexpected	_____
7. train	_____	spelling	_____
8. brake	_____	_____	
9. trail	_____		
10. they	_____		

Challenge Words

11. raise _____

12. plate _____

13. scrape _____

B. Write three list words that rhyme with one another.

1. _____   _____   _____

Six other list words have a rhyming partner. Write them below.

2. _____   3. _____   4. _____

_____   _____   _____

© 2013 Scholastic Education International (S) Pte Ltd ISBN 978-981-07-1363-8

A. Use the list words to complete the letter.

Dear John,

My family went _____ on vacation. We took a _____ to Arizona. My favorite part was riding horses. We followed a _____ into the desert. Suddenly my horse had to _____. He saw a _____ on the trail. The snake was hurt and in _____. I didn't know what to _____. "Stop!" I called. The others _____ their horses stop. _____ saw the snake, too. We used a stick to move the snake under a rock. I hope he'll be okay.

Your friend,

Joe

B. Follow the clues to complete the puzzle.

Across

2. rhymes with **sale**
3. to speak
6. a form of transportation
7. a synonym for **swap**

Down

1. you feel this when you are hurt
2. a list word with an unexpected spelling
4. rhymes with **day**
5. a reptile

Date: _____

*The **long -e** sound can be spelled with the letters **e_e**, **ea** or **ee**.*

A. Read and copy each list word. Circle the letters that make the long -e sound. Then organize the list words by the letters making the long -e sound.

 List Words

			e_e	ee
1.	meet	_____	_____	_____
2.	each	_____	_____	_____
3.	here	_____		_____
4.	read	_____	**ea**	_____
5.	seen	_____	_____	
6.	team	_____	_____	
7.	wheel	_____	_____	
8.	mean	_____	_____	
9.	eve	_____		
10.	sleep	_____		

🏆 Challenge Words

11.	these	_____
12.	easy	_____
13.	please	_____

B. Change one letter in each word to spell a list word. The first one has been done for you.

1. sheep ____sleep____   2. been _____   3. melt _____
4. meal _____   5. tear _____   6. road _____
7. hare _____   8. ewe _____

   © 2013 Scholastic Education International (S) Pte Ltd ISBN 978-981-07-1363-8

Date: _____

Circle ten misspelled words. Write them correctly on the lines below.

A Sleepy Team

Last weak our gymnastics teem met heer. Eech boy and girl had to practice harder than before. We worked as hard as a hamster running on a weel. We did not even have a chance to sleap. At first we thought our coach was meen, but now I have sean what extra work can do for our team. We are all tired, but we are ready for our first gymnastics meet on New Year's Eev. You can rede about it in the newspaper. I hope we do well!

1. _____
2. _____
3. _____
4. _____
5. _____
6. _____
7. _____
8. _____
9. _____
10. _____

Use addition and subtraction to spell each list word.

11. swan – sw + me = _____
12. sell – ll + en = _____
13. help – lp + re = _____
14. she – sh + ev = _____
15. rest – st + ad = _____
16. creep – cr + sl = _____
17. wheat – at + el = _____
18. well – ll + ek = _____
19. itch – it + ea = _____
20. clam – cl + te = _____

Write the challenge word that matches each definition.

21. simple _____

22. used with a request, to show good manners _____

23. used before a plural noun _____

Date: _____

 *The **long -i** sound can be spelled with the letters **i_e**, **igh** or **y**.*

A. Read and copy each list word. Circle the letters that make the long -i sound. Watch out for a word that has an unexpected spelling. Then organize the list words by the letters making the long -i sound.

List Words

			i_e	**y**
1.	sky	_____	_____	_____
2.	time	_____	_____	_____
3.	right	_____	_____	_____
4.	night	_____		_____
5.	cry	_____	**igh**	
6.	wide	_____	_____	
7.	try	_____	_____	
8.	light	_____	_____	
9.	slide	_____		
10.	why	_____		

Challenge Words

11.	while	_____
12.	bright	_____
13.	stripe	_____

B. Circle the word that is spelled correctly.

1.	slyde	slide	2.	try	trie	3.	nite	night
4.	right	ryte	5.	skye	sky	6.	light	lite
7.	wide	wyde	8.	cry	crie	9.	whi	why

 © 2013 Scholastic Education International (S) Pte Ltd ISBN 978-981-07-1363-8

Date: _____

Write the list word that matches each clue.

1. I am the antonym for **day**. I am _____.

2. Children sit on me at the park. I am a _____.

3. I begin with the same sound as **truck**. I am _____.

4. I am used to ask a question. I am _____.

5. I am a synonym for **weep**. I am _____.

6. I am an antonym for **narrow**. I am _____.

7. We rhyme with **bite**. We are _____, _____ and _____.

8. I am always above you. I am the _____.

9. I tell past, present and future. I am _____.

Circle each list word hidden in the puzzle. The words go across, down or diagonally.

a	q	w	t	s	l	i	d	e	c	r
t	t	r	i	d	i	i	s	s	k	w
r	p	i	e	d	i	u	g	b	k	h
y	l	g	m	y	e	w	o	h	i	y
m	f	h	v	e	n	i	g	h	t	s
i	n	t	i	l	h	t	g	c	r	y

Date: _____

> *The **long -o** sound can be spelled with the letters **o_e**, **oa** or **ow**.*

A. Read and copy each list word. Circle the letters that make the long -o sound. Watch out for a word that has an unexpected silent letter. Then organize the list words by the letters making the long -o sound.

 List Words

		o_e	ow
1.	toad	_____	_____	_____
2.	grow	_____	_____	_____
3.	nose	_____	_____	_____
4.	boat	_____		
5.	snow	_____	oa	
6.	broke	_____	_____	
7.	close	_____	_____	
8.	soap	_____	_____	
9.	coat	_____	_____	
10.	know	_____		

🏆 **Challenge Words**

11.	show	_____
12.	wrote	_____
13.	those	_____

B. Can you find all ten list words hidden two times? Circle them.

brocoatknsoapow	noknowplbrokese	boclosewtoadoatn
snowabrokeknow	bogrowboatlosen	clonosegrowocoat
closeknosnowese	knonoseowsoape	toadyowboatnown

Date: _____

Use a list word to complete each analogy.

1. **Bathing suit** is to **summer** as _____ is to **winter**.

2. A **train** is to **tracks** as a _____ is to **water**.

3. A **knob** is to a **door** as a _____ is to a **face**.

4. **See** is to **saw** as **break** is to _____.

5. **Rain** is to **warm** as _____ is to **cold**.

6. A **tiger** is to **mammal** as a _____ is to **amphibian**.

7. **Drink** is to **drank** as _____ is to **knew**.

8. **Shampoo** is to **hair** as _____ is to **body**.

Use the clues to identify the list words. Move the sleds down the hill by circling the answers. The sled that reaches the bottom first is the winner!

9. to get bigger

10. used to smell

11. used to clean

12. knit – it + ow

13. antonym for **open**

14. a type of transportation

15. chow – ch + sn

16. used to keep warm

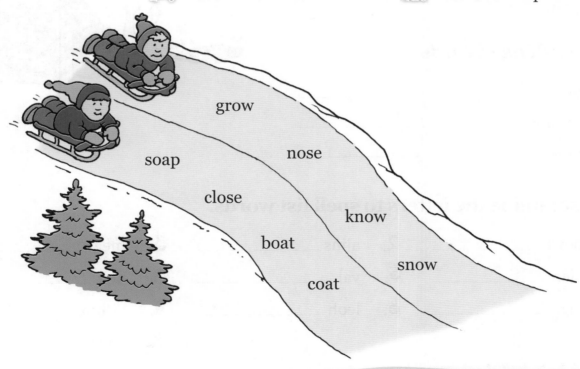

grow

nose

soap

close

know

boat

snow

coat

Date: _____

 Some of the common spellings for **long-vowel** *sounds are:*

a_e	e_e	i_e	o_e
ai, ay	ea, ee	y, igh	oa, ow

A. Read and copy each list word. Circle the letters that make the long-vowel sound. Then organize the list words by their long-vowel sounds.

List Words

1. deep
2. hole
3. ride
4. meal
5. snail
6. blow
7. game
8. lay
9. goat
10. might

long -**a** sound
_____
_____
_____
_____
_____
_____
_____

long -**i** sound
_____
_____

long -**o** sound
_____
_____
_____

long -**e** sound

Challenge Words

11. globe _____
12. became _____
13. smile _____

B. Unscramble the letters to spell list words.

1. bowl _____
2. alins _____
3. mega _____
4. alem _____
5. yal _____
6. deir _____
7. tago _____
8. leoh _____
9. githm _____
10. eped _____

© 2013 Scholastic Education International (S) Pte Ltd ISBN 978-981-07-1363-8

Date: _____

Write four sentences using at least two list words.

1. _____
2. _____
3. _____
4. _____

Crack the code to spell each list word.

1	2	3	4	5	6	7	8	9	10	11	12	13	14	15	16	17
g	a	w	r	s	n	i	l	y	d	p	o	t	b	m	h	e

5. 1–2–15–17

   _____

6. 16–12–8–17

   _____

7. 8–2–9

   _____

8. 15–17–2–8

   _____

9. 1–12–2–13

   _____

10. 10–17–17–11

    _____

11. 15–7–1–16–13

    _____

12. 4–7–10–17

    _____

13. 14–8–12–3

    _____

14. 5–6–2–7–8

    _____

Write the challenge word that belongs in each group.

become, becoming,	map, atlas,	smirk, frown,
_____	_____	_____

Date: _____

 *The **long -u** sound can be spelled with the letters **oo** or **u_e**.*

A. Read and copy each list word. Circle the letters that make the long -u sound. Watch out for a word that has an unexpected spelling. Organize the list words by the letters making the long -u sound.

List Words

		oo	u_e
1. room	_____	_____	_____
2. food	_____	_____	_____
3. tube	_____	_____	_____
4. mule	_____	_____	_____
5. moon	_____		_____
6. rule	_____	unexpected	
7. spoon	_____	spelling	
8. cute	_____	_____	
9. tune	_____		
10. who	_____		

Challenge Words

11. school _____
12. goose _____
13. scooter _____

B. Change one letter in each word to spell a list word.

1. cube _____ or _____   2. zoom _____
3. tube _____   4. why _____   5. role _____
6. spook _____   7. noon _____   8. fool _____
9. male _____

Date: _____

A. Use a list word to complete each sentence.

1. A _____ is a mammal similar to a donkey.

2. There is a _____ baby mule at the zoo.

3. The baby mule gets anxious when he wants _____.

4. He has plenty of _____ to play in his pen.

5. One zoo _____ is that visitors cannot feed the mule.

6. The _____ revolves around Earth.

7. _____ is going to the football game?

8. My baby sister has learned to eat with a _____.

9. Have you heard this _____ before?

10. I found a _____ of toothpaste in my suitcase.

B. Follow the clues to complete the puzzle.

Across

2. rhymes with **groom**
5. a breakfast utensil

Down

1. a question word
3. seen in the night sky
4. bread, fruit, vegetables

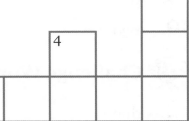

C. Write the challenge word that finishes each analogy.

1. A unicycle has one wheel. A _____ has two wheels.

2. A baby cow is a calf. A baby _____ is a gosling.

3. We play on a playground. We learn in a _____.

Date: _____

When the **long -u** *sound is found at the end of a word, it can be spelled with the letters* **ew** *or* **ue***.*

A. Read each list word. Circle the letters that make the long -u sound. Watch out for a word that has an unexpected spelling. Then organize the list words by the letters making the long -u sound.

List Words

	ew	ue
1. few	_____	_____	_____
2. new	_____	_____	_____
3. true	_____	_____	_____
4. blue	_____	_____	
5. grew	_____	_____	unexpected
6. flew	_____	_____	spelling
7. glue	_____		_____
8. drew	_____		
9. threw	_____		
10. two	_____		

Challenge Words

11. due _____
12. dew _____
13. knew _____

B. Change the first and last letters of each word to spell a list word.

1. grub _____   2. owl _____   3. let _____ *and* _____

4. sled _____   5. club _____ *and* _____

© 2013 Scholastic Education International (S) Pte Ltd ISBN 978-981-07-1363-8

Date: _____

Circle ten misspelled words. Write them correctly on the lines.

A True-Blue Friend

"Today was a great day at school," Mark said as he thrue the
door open. He sat down at the table and took a fue grapes from
the bowl. "We drooe pictures to show the parts of a plant. Before
I could glew my pictures in place, Drew walked by and brushed
them onto the floor. I was so mad! I had to draw tow noow
pictures! Then something pretty cool happened. Matthew came
over and helped me. We flewe through the work together. I grue less angry then."
Mark's mom replied, "Matthew really is a troo-blewe friend."

1. _____ 2. _____ 3. _____
4. _____ 5. _____ 6. _____
7. _____ 8. _____ 9. _____
10. _____

Use addition and subtraction to spell each list word.

11. flag – ag + ew = _____   12. glad – ad + ue = _____

13. net – t + w = _____   14. toe – oe + wo = _____

15. drum – um + ew = _____   16. grip – ip + ew = _____

17. trap – ap + ue = _____   18. fur – ur + ew = _____

19. crew – c + th = _____   20. blob – ob + ue = _____

Write the challenge word that matches the definition.

21. drops of water sometimes found on grass early in the morning _____

22. something owed or expected to arrive _____

23. the past tense of **know** _____

© 2013 Scholastic Education International (S) Pte Ltd   ISBN 978-981-07-1363-8

Date: _____

 *The letters **u**, **oo** and **ou** can all sound like **oo** in **good**.*

A. Read and copy each list word. Circle the letters that make the short -oo sound. Watch for three words that have unexpected spellings. Then organize the list words by the letters that make the short -oo sound.

List Words

		u	ou
1. good	_____	_____	_____
2. book	_____	_____	_____
3. put	_____	_____	_____
4. could	_____		
5. look	_____	**oo**	
6. pull	_____	_____	
7. would	_____	_____	
8. push	_____	_____	
9. foot	_____	_____	
10. should	_____		

Challenge Words

11. stood _____
12. shook _____
13. cookbook _____

B. Circle the word that is spelled correctly.

1. shood   should
2. louk   look
3. put   poot
4. foot   fout
5. cood   could
6. gude   good
7. pul   pull
8. book   booke
9. woud   would
10. puch   push

© 2013 Scholastic Education International (S) Pte Ltd   ISBN 978-981-07-1363-8

Date: _____

Write the list word that matches each clue.

1. I am the antonym for **push**. I am _____.
2. When I am plural, I become **feet**. I am _____.
3. I have a homonym that is spelled as **wood**. I am _____.
4. You use your eyes to do this. This is _____.
5. I am a synonym for **shove**. I am _____.
6. I am a noun. I am made of paper. I am a _____.
7. I am a three-letter word. I am _____.
8. I am less than **great**. I am _____.
9. We rhyme with **good**. We are _____, _____ and _____.

Circle each list word hidden in the puzzle. The words go across, down or diagonally.

g	p	u	s	h	k	w	p	u	t	f
b	p	u	o	h	s	b	l	c	j	o
o	h	c	l	n	o	i	r	o	t	o
o	l	q	v	l	d	u	b	u	o	t
k	w	o	u	l	d	c	l	l	a	k
f	m	e	d	s	g	o	o	d	t	l

Write the challenge word that finishes each exclamation.

10. We _____ on the back of a dolphin!
11. The earthquake _____ the house!
12. This is a great _____!

© 2013 Scholastic Education International (S) Pte Ltd ISBN 978-981-07-1363-8

In some words, two letters work together to make one sound. The two letters are called a **digraph.**

A. Read and copy each list word. Circle the letters that make one new sound. Then organize the list words by the letters that make the new sound.

List Words

			sh	**wh**
1.	wish	_____	_____	_____
2.	chase	_____	_____	_____
3.	shell	_____	_____	
4.	shut	_____		**wh** and **ch**
5.	than	_____	**ch**	_____
6.	chat	_____	_____	
7.	white	_____	_____	
8.	them	_____		
9.	which	_____	**th**	
10.	what	_____	_____	

Challenge Words

11.	there	_____
12.	where	_____
13.	these	_____

B. Can you find all ten list words hidden two times? Circle them.

awshellchwisht	thchasethemack	whshutshchatn
whichthannth	shwhiteafwhatin	chasetwhatente
shutthanewish	prshellenchathir	whichwhitethem

Use a list word to complete each analogy.

1. To trot is to run. To _____ is to talk.

2. Grass is green. Snow is _____.

3. **Him** means one person. _____ means more than one person.

4. A rock is found in the dirt. A _____ is found in the ocean.

5. **High** is the antonym for **low**. _____ is the antonym for **open**.

6. **See** is a homonym for **sea**. _____ is a homonym for **witch**.

7. **Chair** rhymes with **hair**. **Pan** rhymes with _____.

8. To run fast is to scurry. To run after is to _____.

9. Make a play in a game. Make a _____ on a star.

10. **Hat** rhymes with **that**. **Hut** rhymes with _____.

Complete each puzzle with two list words.

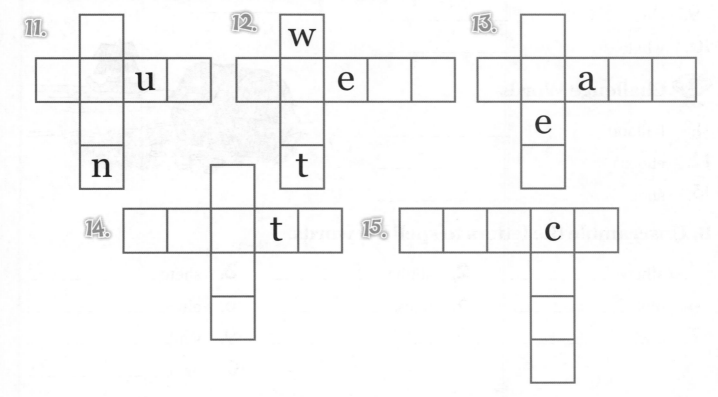

Date: _____

 *In some words two letters work together to make one sound. The **long -u** sound can be spelled with the letters **oo**, **u_e**, **ew** and **ue**. The **short -oo** sound can be spelled with the letters **u**, **oo** and **ou**.*

A. Read and copy each list word. Watch out for a word that has an unexpected spelling. Then organize the list words by the listed sounds.

📝 List Words

		long -u sound as in room	ch, th, wh or sh
1.	bush	_____	
2.	tool	_____	_____	_____
3.	thin	_____	_____	_____
4.	blew	_____	_____	_____
5.	chest	_____		_____
6.	took	_____	short -oo sound as in good	_____
7.	brush	_____		
8.	shape	_____	_____	
9.	clue	_____	_____	
10.	whale	_____		

🏆 Challenge Words

11.	balloon	_____
12.	choose	_____
13.	shoe	_____

B. Unscramble the letters to spell list words.

1. alhew _____
2. sbuhr _____
3. shetc _____
4. olot _____
5. phesa _____
6. eluc _____
7. elwb _____
8. niht _____
9. shub _____
10. okot _____

Riddle time! Use the clues to write each list word in the boxes. When you have finished, the shaded boxes will spell the answer to the riddle.

What has ten letters and runs on petrol?

1. A square is a _____.

2. rhymes with **blue**

3. a part of the body

4. past tense of **take**

5. a hammer

6. a plant

7. antonym for **thick**

8. an ocean animal

9. homonym for **blue**

Write the challenge word that belongs in each group.

sock, boot,	decide, pick,	circus, clown,
_____	_____	_____

Date: _____

 The sound a vowel makes often changes when it is followed by an **r.**

A. Read and copy each list word. Circle the vowel plus r spellings. Watch out for words that have unexpected spellings. Then organize the list words by the number of letters they have.

List Words

three letters

five letters

1. smart _____ _____ _____

2. her _____ _____

3. bird _____ four letters _____

4. more _____ _____

5. curl _____ _____

6. sharp _____ _____

7. were _____ _____

8. first _____ _____

9. hurt _____ _____

10. your _____

Challenge Words

11. morning _____

12. third _____

13. before _____

B. Write a list word that begins with the same sound as the picture.

1. _____

2. _____ *and* _____

3. _____

4. _____

5. _____

6. _____

7. _____

8. _____

Circle ten misspelled words. Write them correctly on the lines.

Kia was given a berd for her eighth birthday. She named her Sweetie. It was the forst pet Kia had ever had. Sometimes Kia's bird would sit on hir shoulder. "Yor bird is really smurt," everyone told Kia. One day Kia and Sweetie wer sitting on the front porch. A wild bird with a cirl on its head landed nearby. Sweetie flew from Kia's shoulder and onto a branch near the wild bird. The wild bird flew away. Kia waited for Sweetie to fly back, but her bird didn't. Sweetie seemed to be hert. Kia lifted Sweetie down and noticed how sharpe the branch was. Kia said, "You can't fly with the wild birds. They have mor experience than you do, Sweetie." The bird seemed to understand and climbed back onto Kia's shoulder.

1. _____ 2. _____ 3. _____ 4. _____
5. _____ 6. _____ 7. _____ 8. _____
9. _____ 10. _____

Follow the clues to play tic-tac-toe. As you find each answer, mark an X or O. Do you get three in a row?

11. I am the antonym for **dull**. Mark an **O**.

12. I begin like the word **birthday**. Mark an **X**.

13. I come before **second**. Mark an **O**.

14. I am the antonym for **less**. Mark an **X**.

15. I show that a girl owns something. Mark an **O**.

16. I am a synonym for **intelligent**. Mark an **X**.

17. I rhyme with **shirt**. Mark an **O**.

18. I rhyme with **her**. Mark an **X**.

19. I describe a vine's stem. Mark an **O**.

her	were	hurt
bird	curl	smart
first	more	sharp

Date: _____

 Two vowels that come together and make one new sound are called a **diphthong**. In some words, vowel combinations come together to make a completely new sound. The letters **ou** and **ow** often make the same sound. For example: **out** and **cow**

A. Read and copy each list word. Circle the ou or ow spelling. Then organize the list words by either ou or ow.

List Words

		ou	ow
1.	how	_____	_____	_____
2.	clown	_____	_____	_____
3.	house	_____	_____	_____
4.	down	_____	_____	_____
5.	now	_____	_____	_____
6.	shout	_____		
7.	about	_____		
8.	town	_____		
9.	count	_____		
10.	our	_____		

Challenge Words

11.	found	_____
12.	crown	_____
13.	mouth	_____

B. Change the last two letters in each word to spell a list word.

| 1. | shore | 2. | abode | 3. | his |
| 4. | couch | 5. | torn | 6. | hound |

Complete the story using each of the list words.

The circus has come to _____! My favorite part is watching the _____ shoot out of the cannon. We all _____ from 10 _____ to zero and then yell, "Blast off!" Then we cover _____ ears because the cannon is loud. You can hear the clown _____ "Wheee..." as he flies over our heads. He flies for _____ two minutes. Then he disappears. "Where is he _____?" everyone asks. Suddenly, the clown jumps out of a dog's _____. "Wow! _____ did he do that?" we all wonder.

Use the clues to identify the list words. Move the clowns along the path by circling the answers. The clown that reaches the circus tent first is the winner.

1. the antonym for **up**
2. Where is _____ dog?
3. a circus performer
4. at this time
5. a synonym for **home**
6. smaller than a city
7. 1, 2, 3 . . .
8. a question word
9. not exact
10. a synonym for **yell**

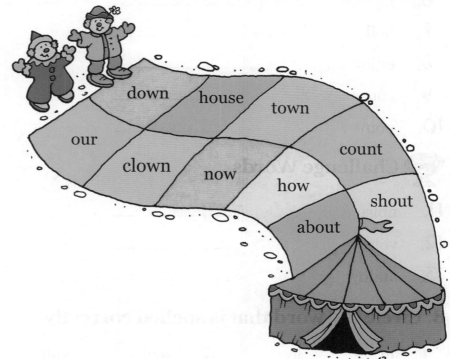

Write the challenge word that completes each question.

11. Has he _____ his notebook yet?
12. Can you talk with your _____ closed?
13. Did you notice all of the jewels in the ancient _____?

Date: _____

The letters **oi** *and* **oy** *often make the same sound. For example:* **oil** *and* **boy**

A. Read and copy each list word. Circle the oi or oy spelling. Then organize the list words by either oi or oy.

List Words

		oi	oy
1. oil	_____	_____	_____
2. boy	_____	_____	_____
3. toy	_____	_____	_____
4. join	_____	_____	_____
5. soil	_____	_____	
6. joy	_____	_____	
7. boil	_____		
8. enjoy	_____		
9. coin	_____		
10. point	_____		

Challenge Words

11. noise _____
12. voice _____
13. annoy _____

B. Circle the word that is spelled correctly.

1. joi	joy	2. soyl	soil	3. toy	toye
4. koin	coin	5. boy	boiy	6. joyn	join
7. enjoy	injoy	8. oil	oyl	9. boyl	boil
10. poynt	point				

© 2013 Scholastic Education International (S) Pte Ltd ISBN 978-981-07-1363-8

Date: _____

Use a list word to complete each analogy.

1. A fish lives in water. A flower lives in _____.

2. **Woman** is to **man** as **girl** is to _____.

3. **Cat** is to **at** as **boil** is to _____.

4. The nose is part of an airplane. The _____ is part of a pencil.

5. Water will freeze when it is cold. Water will _____ when it is hot.

6. **Rough** is the antonym of **smooth**. **Dislike** is the antonym of _____.

7. To separate is to break apart. To _____ is to come together.

8. Sadness is pain. Happiness is _____.

9. A tire is made of rubber. A _____ is made of metal.

10. A dog plays with a bone. A child plays with a _____.

Use the Braille code to spell each list word.

b	c	e	i	j	l	n	o	p	s	t	y

11. ___ ___ ___

12. ___ ___ ___

13. ___ ___ ___ ___

14. ___ ___ ___

15. ___ ___ ___

16. ___ ___ ___ ___

17. ___ ___ ___ ___ ___

18. ___ ___ ___

19. ___ ___ ___ ___

20. ___ ___ ___ ___ ___

Write the challenge word that completes each analogy.

21. **Scream** is a synonym for **yell**. **Bug** is a synonym for _____.

22. You walk with your feet. You sing with your _____.

23. You hear whispers in the library. You hear _____ on the playground.

Date: _____

The letters **aw** make the sound in the word **law**. The letters **all** make the sound in the word **ball**. These are two different sounds.

A. Read and copy each list word. Circle the aw or all spellings. Then organize the list words by either aw or all.

 List Words

		aw	all
1.	tall	_____	_____	_____
2.	jaw	_____	_____	_____
3.	ball	_____	_____	_____
4.	hall	_____	_____	_____
5.	paw	_____		
6.	saw	_____		
7.	call	_____		
8.	draw	_____		
9.	yawn	_____		
10.	fall	_____		

🏆 Challenge Words

11.	dawn	_____
12.	claw	_____
13.	hawk	_____

B. Write a list word that begins with the same letter as the picture.

1. _____

2. _____

3. _____

4. _____

5. _____

6. _____

7. _____

8. _____

9. _____

Write the list word that matches each clue.

1. I am an animal's foot. I am a _____.

2. You do this when you are sleepy. This is a _____.

3. I am part of your face. I am a _____.

4. I am a season called **autumn**. I am _____.

5. I am an antonym for **short**. I am _____.

6. I am the past tense of **see**. I am _____.

7. I am shaped like a sphere. I am a _____.

8. I am the present tense of **drew**. I am _____.

9. I may be part of your school or house. I am a _____.

10. Your mother may do this at dinner time. She may _____ you.

Circle each list word hidden in the puzzle. The words go across, down or diagonally.

r	h	j	p	d	c	f	a	l	l	d
b	t	a	y	p	a	w	b	j	a	r
c	y	b	l	f	l	t	l	a	c	a
d	a	h	c	l	l	y	a	w	l	w
k	w	s	a	w	s	f	s	l	p	l
f	n	e	a	l	l	r	j	p	l	l

Change the last two letters in each word to spell a challenge word.

11. clip

12. hand

13. damp

Date: _____

Throughout the year, see if you can learn all the words on this spelling list.

about	close	foil	lay	pick	slide	took
act	clown	food	light	point	slip	tool
art	clue	foot	lock	pull	small	town
away	coat	fox	look	push	smart	toy
ball	coin	front	made	put	snail	trade
bed	come	frown	map	read	snake	trail
beg	could	game	meal	ride	snow	train
begged	count	girl	mean	right	soap	true
bend	crack	glue	meet	room	sock	try
best	cry	goat	met	rub	soil	tub
bird	curl	good	might	rule	some	tube
black	cut	grew	milk	run	south	tune
blew	cute	grow	miss	running	spoon	turn
blow	deep	hall	mix	sack	spot	two
blue	dot	has	moon	said	stop	went
boat	down	have	mop	saw	straw	were
boil	draw	her	more	say	tall	whale
book	drew	here	mule	seen	tap	what
box	drop	hid	must	send	tapping	wheel
boy	dropped	hole	nest	shape	team	which
brake	dump	horse	new	sharp	tent	white
broke	dust	house	night	shell	than	who
brush	each	how	nose	should	that	why
bump	enjoy	hurt	now	shout	them	wide
bush	eve	jaw	odd	shut	they	wish
call	fall	join	off	sister	thin	with
chase	few	joy	oil	skip	threw	would
chat	first	kick	our	skipping	time	yawn
chest	flag	kiss	pain	sky	tip	yet
clap	flew	know	paw	sleep	toad	your

Fill in the bubble next to the correct answer.

1. Which word rhymes with **shake**?

○ **A**   seed

○ **B**   date

○ **C**   bake

○ **D**   skate

2. Which word rhymes with **seed**?

○ **A**   fear

○ **B**   ate

○ **C**   weed

○ **D**   wait

3. Which word has the **short -a** sound?

○ **A**   bait

○ **B**   clap

○ **C**   made

○ **D**   bay

Fill in the bubble next to the correct answer.

4. Which word has the **long -e** sound?

○ **A**   bench

○ **B**   next

○ **C**   met

○ **D**   feed

5. Which word does NOT have the **short -o** sound?

○ **A**   clock

○ **B**   mop

○ **C**   boat

○ **D**   stop

6. Which word rhymes with **tub**?

○ **A**   was

○ **B**   dump

○ **C**   dust

○ **D**   rub

© 2013 Scholastic Education International (S) Pte Ltd ISBN 978-981-07-1363-8

Fill in the bubble next to the correct answer.

7. Which is the correct spelling of the past tense of **clap**?

○ **A**   clapping

○ **B**   claped

○ **C**   clapped

○ **D**   clapt

8. Which is the correct spelling of the past tense of **drop**?

○ **A**   dropt

○ **B**   droped

○ **C**   dropping

○ **D**   dropped

9. Which word does NOT have the **long -a** sound?

○ **A**   have

○ **B**   hay

○ **C**   snail

○ **D**   made

© 2013 Scholastic Education International (S) Pte Ltd   ISBN 978-981-07-1363-8

Fill in the bubble next to the correct answer.

10. Which answer solves the problem below?

crew − c + th =

- ○ **A**   threw
- ○ **B**   creth
- ○ **C**   thcrew
- ○ **D**   weth

11. Which word is spelled correctly?

- ○ **A**   shood
- ○ **B**   brooke
- ○ **C**   should
- ○ **D**   woud

12. Which word is spelled correctly?

- ○ **A**   puch
- ○ **B**   push
- ○ **C**   coud
- ○ **D**   louk

© 2013 Scholastic Education International (S) Pte Ltd   ISBN 978-981-07-1363-8

Reading Skills

"Reading is fun!" — especially when your child understands how to use key reading skills to make meaning out of the words he or she reads. Good readers set a purpose when reading: to find the main idea, to discover important details, to find the sequence of the story, to compare and contrast story events or characters, to make inferences and predictions, or to draw conclusions. The activities in this section will familiarize your child with these key reading skills so that he or she is equipped to make meaning out of the texts they read.

What To Do

Read the directions on each activity page with your child. Have your child complete the activity. Then check the work together. Answers, when needed, are provided at the back of the book.

When your child reads the nonfiction selections, have him or her answer the questions to test his or her comprehension.

Keep On Going!

Read a book or watch a TV show with your child. At good stopping points ask questions like: *What do you think will happen next? How is that character like or different from other characters in the story? Where does the story take place? Is there a problem? What is it? How is it solved? What have you learned?*

Date: _____

 When you are reading, do you get stuck on words that you don't know? **Context clues** *can help you. Use context clues to figure out what the word is. Think about the other words in the sentence. What clues do they give? Then ask yourself what other word would make sense there.*

What do you think the underlined word means in each sentence below? Circle the meaning that makes sense. Then rewrite each sentence using the meaning instead of the underlined word.

1. My domino has two white <u>pips</u>, and yours has five.

baby dogs   spots   long metal tubes

_____

_____

2. A gray <u>fulmar</u> flew by the cruise ship.

lizard   swordfish   seabird

_____

_____

3. The queen had a beautiful necklace made of <u>jasper</u>.

a green stone   yellow pudding   wet snow

_____

_____

4. My sister is the best <u>flutist</u> in the high-school band.

waitress   runner   flute player

_____

_____

© 2013 Scholastic Education International (S) Pte Ltd ISBN 978-981-07-1363-8

*The **main idea** of a story tells what the whole story is about.*

When you were younger, you learned your ABCs. Letters are the building blocks of words. Words are the building blocks of sentences. We use sentences to communicate our thoughts and feelings. Each letter of the alphabet has at least one sound. Some letters have more than one sound. There are 26 letters in our alphabet. Many of our letters come from alphabets made long ago in faraway places. In fact, the word **alphabet** comes from two words, **alpha** and **beta**, which are the first two letters in the Greek alphabet!

Underline the title that describes the main idea of the story above.

Playing With Blocks   All About Our Alphabet   The Greek Language

Now let's play a game using the alphabet. Read each clue below. Draw a line to the letters that sound like the correct answer.

1. I borrowed some money from your piggy bank. _____ fifty cents.

2. This math is not hard. It's _____.

3. What did the blind man say to the doctor who made him see again? _____

4. What insect makes honey? _____

5. I drank all my milk. Now my glass is _____.

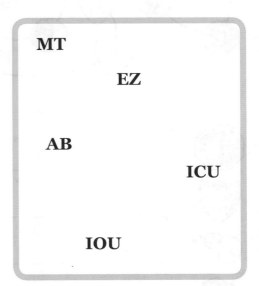

MT

EZ

AB

ICU

IOU

Date: _____

It is good to know that you can call a police officer when you need help. Police officers help find lost children. They direct traffic when there is a problem on the roads. They arrest criminals so that our towns are safe. When people have been in car accidents, police officers come quickly to help them. During floods, fires and tornadoes, they take people to safe places. Sometimes they rescue people who are in danger. Police officers have saved many lives. Think of a police officer as your best friend!

What do you think the main idea of this story is? To find out, read the letters that are connected in the puzzle. Write the letters in order beside the matching shapes.

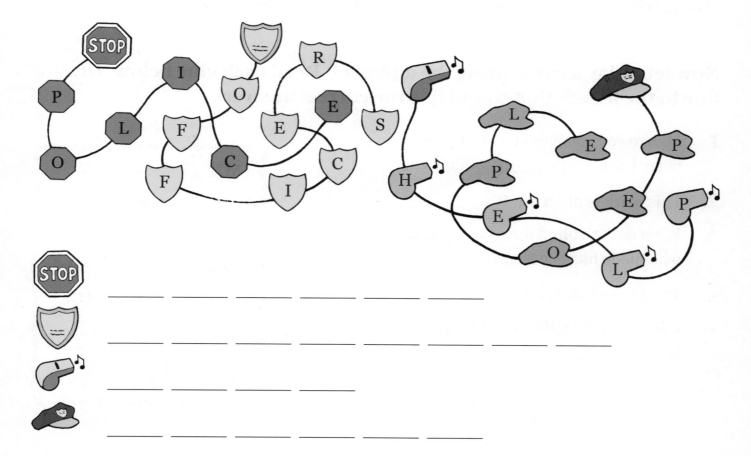

STOP _____ _____ _____ _____ _____ _____ _____

🛡 _____ _____ _____ _____ _____ _____ _____ _____

🎵 _____ _____ _____ _____ _____

🎩 _____ _____ _____ _____ _____ _____

© 2013 Scholastic Education International (S) Pte Ltd ISBN 978-981-07-1363-8

Details *are parts of a story. Details help you understand what the story is about.*

On Saturday, Rachel got up early. Her mom was still asleep, so Rachel made her own breakfast. She put some peanut butter in a bowl. She mixed it with a little honey. Then she stirred in some oatmeal, bran flakes and raisins. It tasted yummy! When Mom got up, she said, "Oh! You made granola!"

Follow the directions below.

1. Circle the word that tells who the main character is.

2. Underline the word that tells what day Rachel made breakfast.

3. Put a box around the word that tells what dish Rachel put the peanut butter in.

4. Put a star (*) by each of the four words that tell what she mixed with the peanut butter.

5. Put a dotted line under the word that describes how it tasted.

6. Put two lines under the word that tells what Mom called the food.

Now find each of the nine words from the activity above in the puzzle below and circle it. The words go across and down.

B	R	A	N	F	L	A	K	E	S	M	H	N	C	L
O	A	T	M	E	A	L	B	K	E	Q	O	J	W	I
W	R	A	I	S	I	N	S	G	R	A	N	O	L	A
L	G	S	A	T	U	R	D	A	Y	P	E	R	D	R
G	R	A	C	H	E	L	Y	U	M	M	Y	F	A	H

Date: _____

Gorillas are the largest apes. They live in the rainforests of Africa. Every morning, they eat a breakfast of leaves, fruit and bark. During most of the day, the adult gorillas take naps. Meanwhile, young gorillas play. They wrestle and chase each other. They swing on vines. When the adults wake up, everyone eats again. When there is danger, gorillas stand up on their hind legs, scream and beat their chests. Every night before it gets dark, the gorillas build a new nest to sleep in. They break off leafy branches to make their beds. Baby gorillas snuggle up to their mothers to sleep.

Find the answers to the puzzle in the story. Write the answers in the squares with the matching numbers.

Across

1. During the day, adult gorillas _____.

3. Gorillas eat leaves, bark and _____.

5. The largest apes are _____.

7. When in danger, gorillas beat their _____.

8. Young gorillas swing on _____.

Down

2. The continent where gorillas live is _____.

4. When young gorillas play, they _____ and chase each other.

6. Baby gorillas snuggle up to their mothers to _____.

© 2013 Scholastic Education International (S) Pte Ltd ISBN 978-981-07-1363-8

Date: _____

 Story events that can really happen are **real.** *Story events that are make-believe are* **fantasy.**

Read each sentence below. If it could be real, circle the picture. If it is make-believe, put an X on the picture.

 Dairy cows give milk.

 The farmer planted pizza and hamburgers.

 The cat said, "Let's go to the dance tonight!"

 The mouse ate the dinner table.

 The hay was stacked in the barn.

 The chickens laid golden eggs.

 The red tractor ran out of gas.

 The newborn calf walked with wobbly legs.

 The goat and the sheep got married by the big tree.

 Two crickets sang "Mary Had a Little Lamb."

 Horses sat on the couch and watched TV.

 Rain made the roads muddy.

 Four little ducks swam in the pond.

 The farmer's wife baked a pumpkin pie.

Grandma Hugfuzzy lived all alone in the country.
She loved to sit on the porch and watch the animals. Every
day, she put food out for the rabbits, raccoons and deer.
She fed the birds with scraps of bread. One terrible, awful,
dreadful day, Grandma Hugfuzzy's house burned down.
Poor Grandma! She had nowhere to go and no one to help
her. She spent the night in an old barn on a bed of hay,
crying herself to sleep. During the night, the animals came
to her rescue. Nine black bears chopped down some trees. A herd of deer carried the wood
on their antlers. Raccoons and rabbits worked all night building a log cabin for Grandma.
Birds flew above the house and nailed the roof in place. When morning came, Grandma
Hugfuzzy was amazed to see what her animal friends had done! She threw a big party for
them that lasted ten years!

**Write a red R on things that are real. Write a purple F on things
that are fantasy.**

a woman feeding animals

deer that carry lumber

a grandmother living alone

animals building a log cabin

a house burning down

bears chopping down trees

crying because her house burned down

a party that lasted ten years

Home Sweet Home

WELCOME

© 2013 Scholastic Education International (S) Pte Ltd ISBN 978-981-07-1363-8

Date: _____

Read each story and answer the questions. Underline the clues that helped you find the answer.

Jake had a lot of homework to do. He added and subtracted until his hand got tired of writing.

1. What kind of homework did Jake have?

spelling   math   reading

After supper, Jake's dad reminded Jake to do his job. Jake went from room to room unloading baskets and cans into a large plastic bag. Then he took the bag out to the garbage can.

2. What was Jake's job?

washing dishes   making the bed   taking out the trash

Jake was tired. He wanted to rest. He went to his bedroom and crawled under the covers.

3. What was Jake doing?

playing a game   going to take a nap   going to eat

Date: _____

 Sequencing *means putting the events in a story in the order that they happened.*

Mia's black cat climbed to the top of a telephone pole and couldn't get down. "Come down, Spooky!" cried Mia. Mia didn't know what to do. She asked her neighbor Mr Carson for help. He was a firefighter before he retired. "What's the matter, Mia?" asked Mr Carson when he saw Mia's tears. "My cat is up on that pole, and I can't get her down!" Mr Carson hugged Mia and said, "I'll call my friends at the fire station to help." A few minutes later, Mia saw the fire truck coming. The firefighters parked near the pole and raised a long ladder to the top. A firefighter climbed the ladder and reached out for Spooky. Just then, Spooky jumped to a nearby tree limb, climbed down the tree and ran into the backyard. Mia said, "Spooky! You naughty cat!" Mr Carson and the firefighters laughed and laughed.

Read the sentences on the ladder. Number them in the order that they happen in the story.

Mia asked Mr Carson for help.

Mr Carson called his firefighter friends.

The firefighters laughed.

A firefighter climbed the ladder.

Mia begged Spooky to come down.

Spooky jumped to a tree and climbed down.

The fire truck came.

Mia scolded Spooky.

Date: _____

You **make inferences** *when you use story details to help you make decisions about what has happened in the story.*

Zolak boarded his spaceship and blasted off from the planet Vartog. He was on a special mission to learn about earthlings. His spaceship landed in a desert. Zolak walked around looking for earthlings, but all he could see were rocks and sand. Then he looked down and saw a dark creature lying down right next to him. In fact, the creature's feet were touching Zolak's feet. Zolak was scared and tried to run away, but everywhere he went, the creature followed. At noon, Zolak realized that the creature had shrunk to a very small size but was still right next to his feet. However, during the afternoon, the dark creature grew longer and longer! Then the strangest thing happened. Night came and the dark creature disappeared!

1. Who do you think the dark creature was?

_____

2. Was the dark creature an earthling?   yes   no

3. Do you think Zolak will give a true report about the earthlings when he returns to Vartog?   yes   no

Why or why not?

_____

Draw a line to match the object to its correct shadow.

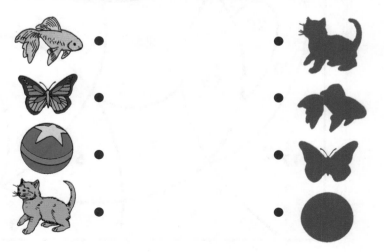

Date: _____

Read each sentence. Then color the numbered space in the picture that matches the number of the correct answer.

He rode his bike.
Who rode it?
1. a boy
2. a girl

Please bait my hook.
What am I doing?
7. fishing
8. playing baseball

Sorry! I broke it.
What could it be?
13. a stuffed animal
14. a crystal vase

Look at the dark cloud.
Where should you look?
19. down
20. up

The lamb lost its mother.
Who is its mother?
21. a sheep
22. a horse

She wore a red hat.
Who wore it?
23. a man
24. a woman

I see a thousand stars.
What time is it?
25. noon
26. night

Let's throw snowballs!
What time of year is it?
3. summer
4. winter

Breakfast is ready!
What time is it?
9. night
10. morning

He's a professor.
What is he?
15. an adult
16. a baby

Run, John, run!
What sport is John in?
5. swimming
6. track

I'm so thirsty.
What will I do?
11. drink something
12. eat something

It won't fit in the car.
What is it?
17. a football
18. a swing set

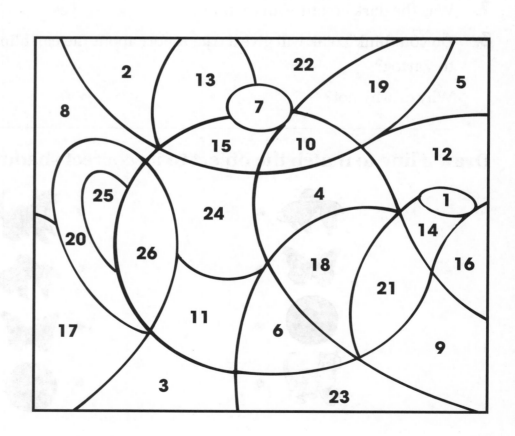

Date: _____

Classifying *means to group together things that are alike. Grouping like things together helps you see how parts of a story are connected and makes the story easier to understand.*

Last summer, Dad, Mom, Tim and Tara went to the beach. They swam, fished, built sandcastles and went sailing. Mom brought a picnic lunch. She spread a blanket on the sand and set out sandwiches, apples and cookies. She brought lemonade in the cooler. Later, Tim and Tara walked along the beach and saw a crab walking sideways. A stray dog was barking at it. A starfish had washed up on the beach, too. Tim threw breadcrumbs up in the air to feed a flock of seagulls. Then the family went home in the evening.

Use the story to find the answers. Fill in the blanks.

2. Picnic Items

_____
_____
_____
_____

1. People Who Went to the Beach

_____
_____
_____
_____

3. What They Did at the Beach

_____
_____
_____
_____

4. Living Things They Saw on the Beach

_____
_____
_____
_____

Date: _____

 Look for similarities when grouping items.

Read each list. Cross out the word that doesn't belong. Then choose a word from the kite that belongs with each list and write it in the blank.

1. grouchy   mad   cheerful   fussy   _____

2. north   away   east   south   _____

3. goat   blue jay   robin   eagle   _____

4. juice   milk   tea   mud   _____

5. hand   toy   foot   head   _____

6. Amazon   Nile   Zambezi   Pacific   _____

7. spinach   cake   cookies   pie   _____

8. glue   bicycle   pencils   scissors   _____

9. card   letter   envelope   marble   _____

Kite words: arm, note, Thames, pudding, lemonade, parakeet, crayons, angry, west

Now read these categories. In each box, write the number from the above list that matches the category.

Birds ☐   Desserts ☐   Bad Feelings ☐

Rivers ☐   Paper ☐   School Supplies ☐

Directions ☐   Body Parts ☐   Drinks ☐

Once upon a time Rita Rabbit was complaining to Diana Duck. "You always have fun, swimming around in the lake. I wish I was a duck. You're lucky." Diana Duck said, "Oh, really? Well, I wish I was a rabbit! You can hop so fast and go so far. I think you're lucky!" Just then the Good Fairy appeared and said, "You are both lucky! I will grant you each your wish." All of a sudden Rita Rabbit became a duck! She waddled to the lake and went for a swim. Diana Duck became a rabbit and hopped down the road as fast as she could go. At the end of the day, Rita was wet and cold. She missed her family. She missed her home in the hole at the bottom of the hollow tree. She wanted to hop over there, but it was too far, and all she could do was waddle. Diana was having trouble, too. She had hopped so far away that she got lost. She began to cry. She wanted to go home to the lake. Just then . . . POOF! The Good Fairy appeared again. She granted Rita and Diana one more wish.

Draw what you think happened when Rita got her second wish.

Draw what you think happened when Diana got her second wish.

Date: _____

Compare *means to look for things that are the same.*
Contrast *means to look for things that are different.*

The second-grade class went to the zoo for a field trip. The next day, the teacher asked the children to write a report about what they learned. Read the two reports below.

Ryan

What I Learned at the Zoo

I learned about the giant tortoise. It was so big that the guide let us sit on its back. Some tortoises live to be over 100 years old! That's older than my grandpa!

The slowest-moving mammal is the three-toed sloth. It hangs from trees and eats fruit. Some sloths sleep more than 20 hours a day. What a lazy animal!

I thought the albino alligator was really cool. It wasn't green. It was completely white all over. It was born that way.

Jessica

What I Learned at the Zoo

The tallest animal on earth is the giraffe. It eats leaves from the tops of the trees. Giraffes come from Africa.

I learned about an albino alligator. It was white instead of green. The guide told us that it was born without the coloring of other alligators.

I saw an owl sleeping in a tree. Owls sleep in the daytime and hunt at night. When they sleep, they don't fall out of the tree because they have sharp claws that lock onto the branch.

Ryan and Jessica each wrote about three animals. Write the names of the animals they wrote about in the correct circles. In the center where the circles overlap, write the name of the animal that they both wrote about.

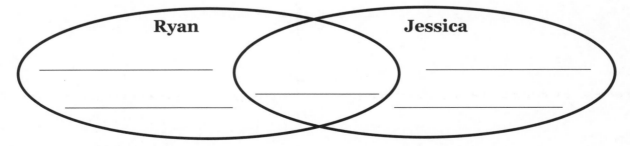

Ryan   Jessica

© 2013 Scholastic Education International (S) Pte Ltd ISBN 978-981-07-1363-8

Kendra and her mom left their house on Oak Street to go to school. Kendra put on her safety belt. About that same time, Lacey and her mom left their house on Maple Street. On the way to school, Lacey bounced up and down on the seat watching her pigtails fly up and down in the mirror. She had forgotten to wear her safety belt. Both moms turned into the school parking lot at the same time, and they crashed into each other! Kendra was not hurt. Her safety belt kept her in her seat. But Lacey fell forward and bumped her head HARD! She cried and cried. She had to go to the hospital and get an X-ray. Lacey got well in a day or two, but she learned an important lesson!

Draw a 😊 in the correct column.

		Kendra	Lacey	Both
1.	driven to school by Mom			
2.	wore a safety belt			
3.	didn't wear a safety belt			
4.	lives on Maple Street			
5.	was in a wreck			
6.	bumped her head			
7.	got an X-ray			
8.	lives on Oak Street			
9.	bounced up and down in the car			
10.	didn't get hurt			
11.	learned a lesson			

Date: _____

Mount Saint Helens is an active volcano in the state of Washington. In 1980, this volcano erupted, spewing hot lava into the air. Explosions caused a huge cloud of dust. This gray dust filled the air and settled on houses and cars many miles away. The thick dust made it hard for people and animals to breathe. The explosions flattened trees on the side of the mountain. The hot rocks caused forest fires. The snow that was on the mountain melted quickly, causing floods and mudslides. Mount Saint Helens still erupts from time to time but not as powerfully as it did in 1980.

Read each phrase below. Write the number of each phrase in the top of the volcano to correctly complete the sentence.

1. Mount Saint Helens erupted,

2. The thick ash made it hard

3. The explosions

4. The hot rocks caused

5. Melting snow caused

6. Because Mount Saint Helens is an active volcano,

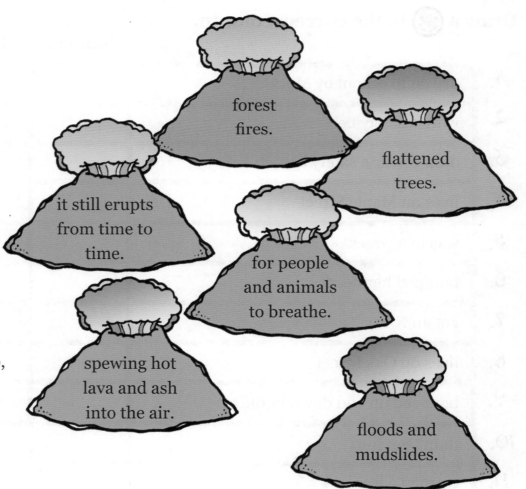

forest fires.

flattened trees.

it still erupts from time to time.

for people and animals to breathe.

spewing hot lava and ash into the air.

floods and mudslides.

© 2013 Scholastic Education International (S) Pte Ltd   ISBN 978-981-07-1363-8

Date: _____

The writing assignment in Ms Daniels' class was to write about someone you admire. Read what one student wrote.

Lunch Lady
by Karen Jackson

I don't know her name. She is one of the workers in our school cafeteria. I just call her Lunch Lady. She's my friend. There are several nice ladies in the cafeteria, but the Lunch Lady is the nicest of all. Every day she smiles at me when I go through the line. She says things like, "Hi Karen! Are you having a good day?" Lunch Lady always remembers that I like chicken nuggets the best. Whenever those are being served, she hands me the chicken nuggets and says, "Look, your favorite!" One day, I tripped and dropped my tray. Food went all over the floor. I was so embarrassed, but Lunch Lady came to my rescue. She helped me pick up the mess, and she told me, "Don't worry about it. It's okay." That made me feel better. Another time, I was at the shoe store with my mom, and I saw Lunch Lady. She gave me a big hug. The reason I admire Lunch Lady is because she is friendly and kind.

Read each sentence. Find the words that are wrong and cross them out. Then above them write the correct word or words that make the sentence true.

1. Karen wrote about Lunch Man.

2. Karen's favorite food is hot dogs.

3. Lunch Lady frowns when Karen comes through the line.

4. When Karen dropped her tray, Miss Daniels helped her.

5. One time, Karen saw the Lunch Lady at the hardware store.

6. Karen admires Lunch Lady because she is friendly and mean.

Treasure Hunt

The city of Whitingham is holding a children's treasure hunt. Children between the ages of seven and twelve may take part. The treasure hunt will take place at Benoit Park on May 31 at 1:00 p.m. Children should meet inside the park's west gate.

Treasure hunters will be given a set of ten clues that lead to the treasure. Children may hunt alone or in teams. The hidden treasure is a box filled with coupons worth $300 in all. The coupons can be used at these places:

Aggie's Ice-Cream Shop
Bike and Skate World
Feather and Fish Pet Store
Gibbons Bowling Alley
Whitingham Roller Rink
Toy City

In case of rain, the treasure hunt will take place on June 7 at 1:00 p.m.

Now answer the following questions.

1. Where will the treasure hunt take place?

    (a)   Whitingham Roller Rink   (b)   Toy City

    (c)   Gibbons Bowling Alley   (d)   Benoit Park

2. What is inside the hidden treasure box?

    _____

3. What will happen to the treasure hunt if it rains on May 31?

    _____

© 2013 Scholastic Education International (S) Pte Ltd ISBN 978-981-07-1363-8

Fill in the bubble next to the correct answer.

1. Which word explains the underlined word in the following sentence?

The <u>data</u> helped to explain how the accident happened.

◯ **A**   certificate

◯ **B**   idea

◯ **C**   information

◯ **D**   results

2. Which sentence tells the main idea about Neil Armstrong's visit to the moon?

◯ **A**   On July 20, 1969, Neil walked on the moon.

◯ **B**   He saw rocks and moon dust.

◯ **C**   Neil Armstrong walks on the moon.

◯ **D**   Millions of people watched this amazing event.

3. Which story event is fantasy?

◯ **A**   The flower spread its beautiful petals.

◯ **B**   The horse ran free on the range.

◯ **C**   It was raining chocolates and donuts.

◯ **D**   Ants attacked our picnic basket.

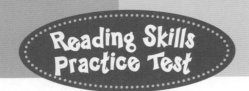

Fill in the bubble next to the correct answer.

4. Which conclusion would you draw about the following event?

Tim worked very hard. When he finished, the car sparkled in the sun.

○ **A**   Tim made breakfast.

○ **B**   Tim washed his car.

○ **C**   He won the basketball game.

○ **D**   He built a car.

5. Which event came first?

○ **A**   Pam finished her homework late at night.

○ **B**   Pam went to school.

○ **C**   She was late to school.

○ **D**   She woke up tired.

6. The temperature was falling. The leaves on the trees were turning gold and orange. What season was it?

○ **A**   summer

○ **B**   winter

○ **C**   spring

○ **D**   fall

© 2013 Scholastic Education International (S) Pte Ltd ISBN 978-981-07-1363-8

Fill in the bubble next to the correct answer.

7. Which of the following words could name the instrument that contains the words north and east?

○ **A**   compass

○ **B**   scale

○ **C**   distance

○ **D**   bay

8. Which of the following does NOT belong in the group?

○ **A**   glider

○ **B**   helicopter

○ **C**   airplane

○ **D**   eagle

9. Which of the following does NOT belong with the others?

○ **A**   tree

○ **B**   leaf

○ **C**   bird

○ **D**   limb

Read the story. Then fill in the bubble next to the correct answer.

Karen has three pet fish. One fish is orange. One fish is black. One fish is red. Karen touches the water and the fish come to the top. Karen feeds her fish every day. She cleans the fishbowl each week. The water is always clean and clear. Karen's fish look very happy swimming in their bowl.

10. A good title for this story would be:

○ **A**   Karen and Her Fish

○ **B**   Karen Has a Red Fish

○ **C**   Fish Love Clean Water

○ **D**   Karen Cleans the Fish Bowl

11. Which is NOT one of the colors of Karen's fish?

○ **A**   red

○ **B**   yellow

○ **C**   black

○ **D**   orange

12. Another word for **clear** is:

○ **A**   dirty

○ **B**   old

○ **C**   clogged

○ **D**   clean

Answer Key

Phonics/Spelling

Page 6
A. Three letters: map, act, has;
Four letters: that, sack, clap, flag, have; Five letters: crack, black;
B. 2. that 3. clap 4. black 5. flag
6. map 7. has 8. sack 9. have

Page 7
A. has, black, that, have, map, clap, sack;
B. 1. act 2. black 3. that 4. crack
5. has 6. sack 7. clap 8. have
9. flag; X wins;

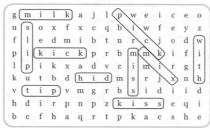

C. 1. stamp 2. stand 3. backpack

Page 8
A. end with t: tent, met, went, nest, yet, best; end with d: send, bed, bend, said;
B. tent/went, met/yet, send/bend, bed/said, nest/best

Page 9
1. tent 2. bend 3. best
4. bed 5. said 6. nest
7. send 8. met 9. went
10. yet 12. tent 13. met
14. bed 15. send 16. said
17. bend 18. yet 19. nest
20. went 21. else 22. bench
23. next

Page 10
A. begin with m: mix, milk, miss; begin with k: kick, kiss; have a p: tip, slip, pick; have an h: hid, with;
B. 1. pick 2. milk 3. kiss 4. tip
5. slip 6. kick 7. hid 8. mix
9. miss

Page 11
1. hid 2. kick, pick 3. milk
4. with 5. mix 6. tip, slip
7. kiss 8. miss 9. sister
10. into 11. trick

```
g [m i l k] a j l [p] w e i c e o
u [s] o x f x c q b [i] w f e y z
f [l] e d m i b t n [r] e j o d [w]
p [i] [k i c k] p r b [m] [m] k i f [i]
l [p] i k x a d v c [i] [m] i r g [t]
k u t b d [h i d] m [s] r j [x] [n] [h]
v [t i p] v m g r b [s] i d i i d
h d i r p n p z [k i s s] e q i
b c f h a q r t p k a c s h e
```

Page 12
A. rhyming pairs: spot/dot, box/fox, sock/lock, mop/stop;
no rhyming partner: odd, off;
B. 1. mop 2. stop 3. sock 4. fox
5. lock 6. spot 7. odd

Page 13
1. off 2. sock 3. mop
4. lock 5. box, fox 6. stop
7. odd 8. dot 9. spot
10. box, sock or lock 11. spot, off
12. fox or box, sock or lock
13. odd, dot 14. stop, mop

Page 14
A. u: rub, bump, cut, dump, must, dust, tub; o: front; o_e: come, some;

B. 1. some 2. must 3. rub
4. bump 5. cut 6. front
7. come 8. dump, dust

Page 15
1. bump, dump 2. rub, tub
3. must, dust 4. come, some
5. some 6. cut 7. rub
8. front 9. dump 10. dust
11. must 12. come 13. tub
14. bump; The red jeep wins.

Page 16
A. no ending: tap, beg, skip, drop, run; -ed ending: begged, dropped; -ing ending: tapping, skipping, running;
B. 1. running 2. begged
3. dropped 4. skip
5. skipping 6. tapping

Page 17
1–4. Review sentences. 5. dropped
6. skip 7. skipping 8. run
9. running 10. drop 11. tap
12. tapping 13. begged 14. beg

Page 18
A. a_e: made, snake, trade, brake; ai: pain, train, trail; ay: say, away; unexpected: they;
B. 1. say, away, they 2. pain, train
3. trade, made 4. snake, brake

Page 19
A. away, train, trail, brake, snake, pain, say, made, they;
B. Across: 2. trail 3. say 6. train
7. trade;
Down: 1. pain 2. they 4. away
5. snake

© 2013 Scholastic Education International (S) Pte Ltd ISBN 978-981-07-1363-8

Page 20

A. e_e: here, eve;   ee: meet, seen,
wheel, sleep;   ea: each, read,
team, mean;

B. 1. sleep   2. seen   3. meet
4. mean   5. team   6. read
7. here   8. eve

Page 21

1. week   2. team   3. here
4. Each   5. wheel   6. sleep
7. mean   8. seen   9. Eve
10. read   11. mean   12. seen
13. here   14. eve   15. read
16. sleep   17. wheel   18. week
19. each   20. team   21. easy
22. please   23. these

Page 22

A. i_e: time, wide, slide;
igh: right, night, light;   y: sky,
cry, try, why;

B. 1. slide   2. try   3. night
4. right   5. sky   6. light
7. wide   8. cry   9. why

Page 23

1. night   2. slide   3. try
4. why   5. cry   6. wide
7. right, light, night   8. sky
9. time

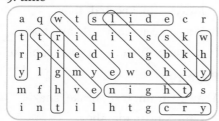

Page 24

A. o_e: nose, broke, close;   ow:
grow, snow, know;   oa: toad,
boat, soap, coat;

B. coat, soap;   know, broke;
close, toad;   snow, know, broke;
grow, boat;   nose, grow, coat;
close, snow;   nose, soap;   toad,
boat

Page 25

1. coat   2. boat   3. nose
4. broke   5. snow   6. toad
7. know   8. soap   9. grow
10. nose   11. soap   12. know
13. close   14. boat   15. snow
16. coat; Sled on right wins.

Page 26

A. long -a: snail, lay, game;
long -e: deep, meal;
long -i: ride, might;
long -o: hole, blow, goat;

B. 1. blow   2. snail   3. game
4. meal   5. lay   6. ride
7. goat   8. hole   9. might
10. deep

Page 27

1–4. Review sentences;
5. game   6. hole   7. lay
8. meal   9. goat   10. deep
11. might   12. ride   13. blow
14. snail; became, globe, smile

Page 28

A. oo: room, food, moon, spoon;
u_e: tube, mule, rule, cute, tune;
unexpected: who;

B. tube, cute
2. room   3. tune   4. who
5. rule   6. spoon   7. moon
8. food   9. mule

Page 29

A. 1. mule   2. cute   3. food
4. room   5. rule   6. moon

7. who   8. spoon   9. tune
10. tube;

B. 1. who   2. room   3. moon
4. food   5. spoon;

C. 1. scooter   2. goose   3. school

Page 30

A. ew: few, new, grew, flew, drew,
threw;   ue: true, blue, glue
unexpected: two;

B. 1. true   2. two   3. few, new
4. flew   5. blue, glue

Page 31

1. threw   2. few   3. drew
4. glue   5. two   6. new
7. flew   8. grew   9. true
10. blue   11. flew   12. glue
13. new   14. two   15. drew
16. grew   17. true   18. few
19. threw   20. blue   21. dew
22. due   23. knew

Page 32

A. u: put, pull, push;   ou: could,
would, should   oo: good, book,
look, foot;

B. 1. should   2. look   3. put
4. foot   5. could   6. good
7. pull   8. book   9. would
10. push

Page 33

1. pull   2. foot   3. would   4. look
5. push   6. book   7. put   8. good
9. could, would, should
10. stood   11. shook   12. cookbook

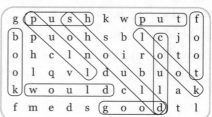

Page 34

A. sh: wish, shell, shut; wh: white, what; ch: chase, chat; th: than, them; wh and ch: which;

B. shell, wish; chase, them; shut, chat; which, than; white, what; chase, what; shut, than, wish; shell, chat; which, white, them

Page 35

1. chat   2. white   3. them
4. shell   5. shut   6. which
7. than   8. chase   9. wish
10. shut   11. than, shut
12. what, shell   13. them, chase
14. wish, white   15. chat, which

Page 36

A. long -u: tool, clue, blew; short -oo: bush, took;   ch, th, wh or sh: thin, chest, shape, whale, brush;

B. 1. whale   2. brush   3. chest
4. tool   5. shape   6. clue
7. blew   8. thin   9. bush
10. took

Page 37

1. shape 2. clue 3. chest 4. took
5. tool   6. bush 7. thin 8. whale
9. blew; Answer to riddle:
automobile; shoe, choose, balloon

Page 38

A. three letters: her; four letters: bird, more, curl, were, hurt, your;   five letters: smart, sharp, first;

B. 1. smart   2. hurt, her   3. first
4. were   5. bird   6. curl
7. sharp   8. more

Page 39

1. bird   2. first   3. her
4. your   5. smart   6. were

7. curl   8. hurt   9. sharp
10. more   11. sharp   12. bird
13. first   14. more   15. her
16. smart   17. hurt   18. were
19. curl; O wins

her	✗	hurt
bird	curl	smart ✗
first	✗ more	sharp

(her circled, bird circled, curl circled, first circled, more circled, sharp circled; X on were, smart, more positions)

Page 40

A. ou: house, shout, about, count, our; ow: how, clown, down, now, town;

B. 1. shout   2. about   3. how
4. count   5. town   6. house

Page 41

town, clown, count, down, our, shout, about, now, house, how;

1. down   2. our   3. clown
4. now   5. house   6. town
7. count   8. how   9. about
10. shout; Clown on left wins.
11. found   12. mouth   13. crown

Page 42

A. oi: oil, join, soil, boil, coin, point; oy: boy, toy, joy, enjoy;

B. 1. joy   2. soil   3. toy   4. coin
5. boy 6. join 7. enjoy 8. oil
9. boil 10. point

Page 43

1. soil   2. boy   3. oil   4. point
5. boil   6. enjoy 7. join 8. joy
9. coin 10. toy 11. oil 12. coin
13. boil 14. toy 15. boy 16. soil
17. enjoy 18. joy 19. join 20. point
21. annoy 22. voice 23. noise

Page 44

A. aw: jaw, paw, saw, draw, yawn; all: tall, ball, hall, call, fall;

B. 1. saw   2. jaw   3. draw
4. fall   5. call   6. ball
7. hall   8. paw   9. yawn

Page 45

1. paw   2. yawn   3. jaw
4. fall   5. tall   6. saw
7. ball   8. draw   9. hall
10. call   11. claw   12. hawk
13. dawn

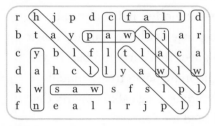

Pages 47–50

1. C 2. C 3. B 4. D 5. C 6. D
7. C 8. D 9. A 10. A 11. C 12. B

Reading Skills

Page 52

1. spots   2. seabird
3. a green stone   4. flute player;
Review Sentences

Page 53

Title: All About Our Alphabet;
1. IOU 2. EZ 3. ICU 4. AB 5. MT

Page 54

POLICE OFFICERS HELP PEOPLE

Page 55

1. Rachel   2. Saturday   3. bowl
4. honey, oatmeal, bran flakes and
raisins   5. yummy   6. granola

(Word search grid: BRANFLAKES, OATMEAL, RAISINS, GRANOLA, SATURDAY, RACHEL, YUMMY)

Page 56

1. nap   2. Africa   3. fruit
4. wrestle   5. gorillas   6. sleep
7. chests   8. vines

Page 57

Circle: cow, hay, tractor, ducks, calf, mud, pumpkin pie;   X: cat; goat and sheep, horse, pizza and hamburger, mouse, golden eggs, crickets

Page 58

R: a woman feeding animals; a house burning down; a grandmother living alone; crying because her house burned down
F: deer that carry lumber; bears chopping down trees; animals building a log cabin; a party that lasted ten years

Page 59

1. math; added and subtracted
2. taking out the trash; unloading baskets and cans into a large plastic bag, took the bag out to the garbage can
3. going to take a nap; He wanted to rest. He went to his bedroom and crawled under the covers.

Page 60

1. Mia begged Spooky to come down.
2. Mia asked Mr Carson for help.
3. Mr Carson called his firefighter friends.
4. The fire truck came.
5. A firefighter climbed the ladder.
6. Spooky jumped to a tree limb and climbed down.
7. Mia scolded Spooky.
8. The firefighters laughed.

Page 61

1. his shadow   2. no   3. Review child's opinion;   Review that the objects are matched to the correct shadows.

Page 62

Color: 1, 4, 6, 7, 10, 11, 14, 15, 18, 20, 21, 24, 26 (teapot)

Page 63

1. Dad, Mom, Tim, Tara
2. sandwiches, apples, cookies, lemonade
3. swam, fished, built sandcastles, went sailing
4. crab, stray dog, starfish, seagulls

Page 64

1. cheerful; angry   2. away; west
3. goat; parakeet   4. mud; lemonade
5. toy; arm   6. Pacific; Thames
7. spinach/pudding
8. bicycle/crayons
9. marble/note;
   Birds: 3, Desserts: 7, Bad Feelings: 1, Rivers: 6, Paper: 9, School Supplies: 8, Directions: 2, Body Parts: 5, Drinks: 4

Page 65

Check drawings for reasonable predictions.

Page 66

Ryan: giant tortoise, three-toed sloth; Both: albino alligator; Jessica: giraffe, owl

Page 67

1. Both   2. Kendra   3. Lacey
4. Lacey   5. Both   6. Lacey
7. Lacey   8. Kendra   9. Lacey
10. Kendra   11. Lacey

Page 68

1. spewing hot lava and ash into the air.
2. for people and animals to breathe.
3. flattened trees.
4. forest fires.
5. floods and mudslides.
6. it still erupts from time to time.

Page 69

1. Man; Lady
2. hot dogs; chicken nuggets
3. frowns; smiles
4. Miss Daniels; Lunch Lady
5. hardware; shoe
6. mean; kind

Page 70

1. d   2. coupons worth $300
3. It will take place on June 7.

Pages 71–74

1. C   2. A   3. C   4. B
5. A   6. D   7. A   8. D
9. C   10. A   11. B   12. D

SCHOLASTIC Learning Express™

Congratulations!

I,

_____

am a Scholastic Superstar!

Paste a photo or draw a
picture of yourself.

I have completed Phonics and Reading Skills L2.

Presented on _____